A Garden Love Story

Charleston, SC
www.PalmettoPublishing.com

A Garden Love Story
Copyright © 2022 by Charlie L. Jones

Hardcover ISBN: 979-8-8229-0157-5
Paperback ISBN: 979-8-8229-0158-2
eBook ISBN: 979-8-8229-0159-9

A Garden Love Story

A Parable of the Faith Journey to Marriage

CHARLIE L. JONES

Dedication

To my late parents, Mr. Charles Jones Jr. and Nelvina Rice Jones, who were married for over twenty years and had seven children. They were farmers who instilled in us the foundation for success, a good work ethic, a healthy respect for authority, a determination to obtain a good education, and most importantly, a foundation of giving reverence to God. As a child, I can remember asking my dubious dad questions about life, many of which he couldn't give definitive answers to, so he would grunt and shake his head and say, "Boy, that's all in life." If I insisted on a response or asked other dubious questions, he would say, "Just keep living!" I can remember him observing my siblings in the yard and me playing with our friends, and after we finished playing, he would sometimes ask us to do a chore. He would look at us as we reluctantly performed the task, slowly shake his head as if he were wondering about something, and mutter softly to himself, saying, "You're living the best years of your life."

On the other hand, Mom was more of a disciplinarian; if I asked her dubious questions about life, she would respond by saying, "You'll have to ask God that!" Mom believed that to "spare the rod was to spoil the child" Prov. 23:13–14 NKJV. She prepared us for life by assigning Bible scriptures for us to read and memorize. She would assign a different number of verses to each of us. She would choose the time frame for the verses to be memorized but allow us to pick our verses. At the time that she specified, we would gather around her and give her our lists of Bible verses. She would recite the chapter and verse, and we would quote the associated scripture, and vice versa. She would sometimes motivate us by increasing the number of verses without increasing the time frame for them to be memorized. She believed that you should "train up a child in the way he should go, and when he is old, he will not depart from it" Prov. 22:6 NKJV.

Time has passed, and Mom and Dad are no longer here. I am sixty-six years old, so God has allowed me to "keep living." I have lived long enough and have experienced enough in my life to know that things happen that I may never understand, but I believe that it's all in God's plan. Through my life trials, I have learned to take my troubles to the Lord in prayer, and although I have a good education, I know that "the fear of the Lord is the beginning of wisdom, and to depart from evil is understanding" Job 28:28 NKJV

Thanks, Dad and Mom, for providing the foundation for lessons that would be well learned in time.

The flowers appear on the earth; The time of singing has come,
And the voice of the turtledove is heard in our land.
—Song of Solomon 2:12 (NKJV)

Earth
Laugh In
Flowers

(Ralph Waldo Emerson)

TABLE OF CONTENTS

Introduction

Jesus in his earthly ministry was a storyteller. He was filled with the Holy Spirit and had wisdom to simplify profound spiritual truths or parables, in a manner in which people could understand. He could take two objects and place them side by side for the purpose of comparing them in a manner to teach biblical principles. Sometimes he would begin his parable in the form of an analogy, such as "The Kingdom of Heaven is like a landowner" (Matt. 20:1 NKJV), or he would provide examples from day-to day life to convey spiritual truth, such as "Nor do they light a lamp and put it under a basket" (Matt. 5–15 NKJV). Many heard his parables, but some of the hearers were confused as to their spiritual meaning. His parables gave revelation or light to those who had a spiritual hunger or thirst to understand them. Conversely, they intensified the ignorance, or revealed the hypocrisy, of those who were in opposition to the gospel.

Jesus could express in a few words spiritual truths that baffled the religious scholars of the days: "Blind guides who strain out a gnat and swallow a camel" (Matt. 23:24 NKJV). Some of his parables were so simple that a layperson could understand: "For you cleanse the outside of the cup and dish, but the inside they are full of extortion and self- indulgence" (Matt. 23:25 NKJV). Oftentimes, even Jesus disciples had difficulty understanding his parables, but when he was alone with them, he would reveal their meanings. The key to understanding the parables of Jesus is to understand that Jesus was part of the Christian doctrine known as the Trinity: the Father, the Son, and the Holy Ghost.

And the three are One.
—1 John 5:7 NKJV

The key to accessing the One is through faith. Sometimes the way faith grows is through life trials or circumstances. It is usually at the point when all options have been exhausted. It is at this point where the seed of faith can grow; then we reach a place of surrender. Jesus can even count this as faith. (Reference Mark 5:24–34 NKJV, healing the woman with the hemorrhage.)

We live in an ambiguous society in which good is described as "bad" and bad is described as "good" (reference Isa. 5:20–21 NKJV). For example, the words *swagger* and *swag* are deemed as desirable qualities in choosing a mate. The word *swagger* is defined as (1) "to walk with a conceited swing or strut" or (2) to "boast, brag." The word *swag* is defined as "stolen goods; loot." (Webster's Dictionary) This ambiguity is reflected in relationships in terms of double standards, lack of commitment, and poor communication.

Sometimes it seems that there are no rules or that everyone makes up their own self-serving rules. In matters of love, everybody is looking for that special someone. They are searching for their soulmate. The question is: How do you find that special someone who is right for you in a world of ambiguity? No one is perfect, and there is no single person perfect for anyone. Jesus gives us free will to choose our mate. He also gives us a choice of whether to seek his counsel in choosing a mate or rely on our own methods. A long-lasting relationship starts with a solid foundation. Jesus gave a parable that emphasized the need to make good choices and to build one's house or relationships on a rock or a firm foundation (reference the man who built his house on sand and the one who built his house on the rock; Matt. 7:24–26 NKJV. If you allow God to be your soulmate, then he will help you choose a helpmate. Making good choices begins with establishing a personal relationship with God.

The inspiration for writing *A Garden Love Story: A Parable of the Faith Journey to Marriage* happened while I working in my garden, the place where I find solace and where I meditate on the word of God. My thought processes were as follows:

1. Humans and vegetables were created by God.
2. Humans have physical features, emotional sensitivities, and varying personalities.
3. Vegetables have vitamins, minerals, and physical characteristics.
4. Adam and Eve were the first (spiritually) married couple, and they resided in the Garden of Eden.

A Garden Love Story: A Parable of the Faith Journey to Marriage resulted from giving human characteristics to vegetables and trying to answer the question, "If vegetables were given a choice of whom to marry, on what criteria would they make their decisions?" The answer for humans is to establishing a personal relationship with God and seeking his guidance prior to making the commitment of marriage. The answer for vegetables is to abide in the vine (reference the Parable of True Vine, John 15:1–7 NKJV). The foundation for *A Garden Love Story* is based on the aforementioned parable and the following scriptures:

Charm is deceitful and beauty is passing, But a woman who fears the Lord,
is to be praised.
—Proverbs 31:30 NKJV

The fear of the Lord is the beginning of wisdom, and the knowledge of the Holy One is understanding.
—Proverbs 9:10 NKJV

Preface

Primary audience: Parents and adolescents who want to learn to build relationships based on biblical principles. This book is a must-read for adults who are looking for long-term relationships or those who are in a relationship and want to know whether he or she "is the right one" based on spiritual compatibility.

A Garden Love Story is a parable in the form of a children's story. It can be used as a pre-marital counseling tool. The story serves as a transition from the "happily ever after" stories of marriage that we enjoyed as children to one based on a spiritual foundation. It is the story of a cabbage who resides in a garden with other vegetables. Daisy Cabbage Head is a cabbage in Godfather Goodson's garden who has reached the age of courtship and is looking for a relationship that may lead to marriage. Her dilemma is how to choose the best helpmate, given all the suitors in the garden. In her journey to find her helpmate, she realizes that her heart has to be cultivated by her gardener to receive the seed of faith. She learns that she must first grow in her relationship with him and be well grounded in faith to make the best decisions.

The lessons learned by Daisy in choosing her mate apply to humans who are seeking long-term relationships. The book has many facets. It can be read to children as a children's story and provide instructions to adolescents and adults to look beyond physical appearance or social status, and accomplishments of a person and allow God to let them see their spiritual essence. The story can serve as a guide to adults who are looking for a partner or those who have been divorced and may be ready to start over. Most importantly, it can help you to see the flaws in yourself and serve to plant the seed of faith to ask God's guidance in choosing a mate. Putting God first in our lives is the best way to ensure that our relationships can stand the trials of life and the test of time.

A Garden Love Story stresses the need for healthy lifestyles in terms of mind (emotional), body (nutritional), and soul (spiritual). The story combines the use of figurative language techniques such as simile, personification, allegory, humor, and metaphors to improve cognitive flexibility in problem solving and decision making. Scriptures and proverbs from the Bible are used in sections of the story to accentuate the stages of spiritual maturity of the main character or to sum up that section from a spiritual perspective. Readers should read each section of the book and then answer corresponding questions in the "Veggie Soup" section to project their relationship or circumstances on to the story. Role reversal is used to make the story gender friendly and to address role ambiguities and double standards in courtship. The "Food for Thought" sections are for the reader to write their thoughts about issues to discuss with their partner or seek biblical counseling. The "Gumbo" section of the book adds the meat to the soup; it encourages you to analyze the type of relationship you have. It demonstrates that even in a tumultuous marriage, trials are sometimes the soil in which faith grows. Difficult circumstances may provide the perfect soil for the heart to be pricked to receive the seed of faith. The Parables in Pictures section are photographs from nature that have the essence of faith. They may be useful in facilitating openness in communication between you and your partner as you share your personal experiences and assess your spiritual growth. All things work for the good for those who love the Lord. *A Garden Love Story* is the companion to the book entitled *Growing a Successful Marriage through Faith*, which is based on an actual marriage case study.

The setting for story is in Field Town in Mr. Goodson's Garden. Mr. Goodson is synonymous with Jesus (God's Good Son). Other characters include Reverend Holyfield (the Holy Spirit), Godfather Goodson (God the Father), and Grace Goodson (God's grace through his Son, Jesus). Most of the characters are vegetables. All have nutritional value, and some even have impressive physical features. Except for Godfather Goodson and Reverend Holifield, all the characters have flaws, including the main character, Daisy Cabbage Head. Each vegetable represents a personality type of someone you may meet or may consider as a partner for a long-term relationship.

Daisy is young and impressionable. She has reached her salad days (the age of courtship) and wants to find someone with whom she can build a relationship that may eventually lead to marriage. She has a dilemma. How can she decide "who is ripe for the picking," or who would make her a good husband? The theme of the story is that successful long-term relationships start with an examination of your relationship with God. All things are possible if the Holy Spirit is your guide. *A Garden Love Story* is also a nonthreatening means to address issues relevant to children, such as bullying, respecting authority figures, and self-esteem. It can also be used to plant the seed for better nutritional choices and promote a love for gardening.

* Metaphorically speaking, a Cabbage Head refers to a person whose problem solving is rooted in the lust of the flesh, the deceitfulness of riches, and the pride of life (as was with Adam and Eve after they disobeyed the instructions of God)—a person lacking spiritual insight.

CHAPTER 1

Life in the Garden of Mr. Godfather Goodson

Thunder, lightning, intense heat, and rain are some of the hazards in the life of cabbages in the garden of Godfather Goodson. To Daisy, these were just minor inconveniences in comparison to the destruction left by the menacing pests, the butterflies. The butterflies invaded their privacy by leaving them the care and responsibilities for their eggs without providing instructions on how to care for them or groceries to feed them. The eggs hatched into thriving caterpillars,

eating them out of house and home and leaving their beautiful green foliage filled with holes. Adding insult to injury, the caterpillars transformed into butterflies and flew away without giving notice of their departure or displaying a show of gratitude.

Miss Daisy Cabbage Head always complained about the butterflies, but secretly she envied them. She was jealous of their ability to fly and of other freedoms she felt they enjoyed. She could imagine butterfly couples flying to Italy to get married or line dancing in midair during their courtship. Daisy's head would steam with passion as she imaged what it would be like to be a butterfly. She envied their carefree lives and options for courtship.

"Who am I kidding? I must be out of my head. I'm grounded!" is what she would say to herself as she returned to consciousness from her daydream. Daisy, with her large melon head and full-figured, crispy roughage, was good for digestive health. She was full of vitamins A and K and antioxidants. Daisy knew this, but she wanted to be more than just the star attraction in someone's vegetable soup bowl. She wanted to be an adult, and to do this, she realized that she needed to turn over a new leaf. Daisy would ask her parents dubious questions like "Why was I born?" and "Why is my life so hard?" and "Why do other veggies get what they want, and I never do?" Her parents, good Christians that they were, could not give her definitive answers, and that frustrated Daisy. She felt they should know the answers because they had been married for many seasons.

Daisy was now on her twentieth day of a ninety-five-day season and felt that her time was running out: "Foolishness is bound up in the heart of a child; the rod of correction will drive it far from him." (Prov. 22:15 NKJV). Her father, Clyde Cabbage Head, and mother, Bonnie Cabbage Head, had two daughters. Daisy's older sister was married to Mr. Spinach. Mr. Spinach was rich in vitamins A and K and essential in weight reduction and red blood cell production. He was a strong leader but a loner because he had a foul mouth and liked to tell distasteful jokes. Daisy's sister and Mr. Spinach had two children, who were both in jail, one for mugging a moth and the other for pickpocketing a peanut.

Even a child is known by his deeds, Whether what he does is pure and right.

—Proverbs 20:11 NKJV

CHAPTER 2

The Greatest Love Story Ever Told—The First Marriage

Daisy's parents thought Daisy's ideas of love were for the birds. They thought her ideas consisted of birds, bees, flowers, and trees, which amounted to apple pie in the sky. Daisy spent most of her time reading romance novels and gossip columns published in the Garden Post Inquirer, a weekly publication by those gabby grapevine reporters. The publication spread gossip and vicious rumors about the affairs of celebrity stars as well as couples in the garden. Daisy's parents wanted her to be more receptive to their teaching, so they told her the greatest love story ever told; it was the story of the first marriage, the marriage of Adam and Eve. The story had been passed down through generations. They told her that after Godfather Goodson created the world, he created the first humans, Adam and Eve. He made them out to the same bone-flesh mixture, so they were perfect for each other. They were so perfect that the first words from Adam's mouth when he saw her were: "*This is now bones of my bones and flesh of my flesh; She shall be called Woman, because she was taken out of Man.*" Gen. 2:23 NKJV It was a miracle; the perfect couple. It was love at first sight.

Adam and Eve were immediately bonded in holy matrimony by Godfather Goodson. As a wedding gift, Godfather Goodson gave them dominion over everything he created and sent them off on a lovely honeymoon to the Garden of Eden. Initially, things were indeed perfect there. He made them caretakers of the garden so they could work together, have ideal communication, and bond with nature. Nature was Godfather Goodson's handwriting; it declared his glory so that even when he was not physically present, they could feel his love and protection. They could communicate in perfect harmony. As they worked in the garden, they could meditate on the things of Godfather Goodson. There were garden parties of praise as they sang and were in perfect harmony with mustards, collards, and other vegetables in the garden.

How wonderful it was to wake up every morning surrounded by roses, morning glories, and honey bears alone with other creatures, all awaiting your command. Things were indeed very good in the garden. One day Godfather Goodson took them on a walk there. He gave them instructions on how to maintain a harmonious relationship with him, with each other, and with nature. Godfather Goodson showed them two trees, the Tree of Life and the Tree of the Knowledge of Good and Evil. He instructed them to eat from the Tree of Life so that they may continue to maintain the bond with him, with each other, and with nature. He told them that if they were obedient to his instructions, in time they would receive spiritual gifts that their hearts couldn't even imagine.

On the other hand, he warned them not to eat from the tree next to it, the Tree of the Knowledge of Good and Evil. He told them that although it seemed good to the eye and seemed suitable for food, on the day they ate of the tree, they would surely die. He said their bond with him and each other would be broken, and on that day, they would surely die.

And it came to pass that Adam and Eve were courted by a suitor with malicious intent. He was subtle in his approach; he caused Adam and Eve to question the instructions and faithfulness of Godfather Goodson. He told them that they misunderstood Godfather Goodson's instructions. He infected their minds by making them false promises of a better life. He told them they could make their own decisions and promised they could become like gods if they ate from the forbidden tree. Adam and Eve saw that the Tree of the Knowledge of Good and Evil was good for food. It was pleasant to the eye and desirable for making one wise, so they fell prey to the imaginations of their hearts. They yielded to temptation, disobeyed the instructions of Godfather Goodson, and ate of the forbidden tree. At the moment, their marital bond, their bond with nature, and their bond with Godfather Goodson were broken.

As a result of their disobedience, their honeymoon ended abruptly, and they reaped what they sowed. Adam and Eve were exiled from the Garden of Eden, never to return. Unfortunately, others also suffered, and even the ground was cursed. As dismal as the circumstances were, the story had a happy ending. Godfather Goodson remained faithful and was willing to give them another chance if they confessed their sins. They chose, however, to maintain their pride. Instead of taking responsibility for their transgression, they were filled with pride. They blamed each other and the suitor for their disobedience. They wanted to be more than just caretakers of a garden; they wanted to be like gods and rule their worlds. Godfather Goodson granted their wish. They were driven from the Garden of Eden into a fool's paradise, a dog-eat-dog world—a world of choices. Since they had no spiritual guidance, they became competitors instead of partners, inmates instead of helpmates. In their new world, their problem-solving strategies were grounded in the lust of the flesh, the deceitfulness of riches, and the pride of life. They had a chaotic family life and broken bonds with each other, nature, and Godfather Goodson. They passed their rebellious nature on to their offspring, Cain and Abel. They showed favoritism between their children to the point at which their oldest son, Cain, killed his brother Abel out of anger and jealousy. The crime was so gruesome that the ground cried out for justice.

Godfather Goodson loved Adam and Eve and the world so much. He sent his only begotten son, Grace Goodson, into the world to pay the price for their disobedience by dying on the cross. This was the price to redeem the world from the suitor and to restore the bond with him and with marriage. The suitor was paid in full through the death and resurrection of Grace Goodson. Sin would no longer have dominion over them. They were given another chance to obey (through faith).

For God so loved the world that He gave His only begotten son, that whosoever believes in Him should not perish but have everlasting life.

—John 3:16 NKJV

Grace Goodson demonstrated his love toward them and future generations in that while they were still (sinners), he gave his life that we may have another opportunity to eat from the Tree of Life and restore the bonds that were broken. He required only one thing—that they believe. Through his example of faithfulness, sacrifice, and forgiveness, he demonstrated what a happy marriage should be. He said that a man should love his wife as himself and that wives should submit to their husbands as to the Lord. He painted this picture of a marriage that is bonded with him: "*Your wife shall be like a fruitful vine in the very heart of your house, your children like olive plants all around the table, Behold thus shall the man be blessed who fears the Lord*" (Ps. 128:3–4 NKJV)

Daisy didn't want to turn out like Adam and Eve nor her parents. In Daisy's parents attempt to teach her about life, they would recite proverbs to her, such as "Life is not a bowl of cherries," "You can't tell a veggie by its *ABCs*," "Don't cry over spilled soup," and "Don't buy an apple if the salesman is a worm." And, yes, their favorite: "A hard head will carry a soft bottom, so don't be a cabbage head." All their teaching, however, went in one of Daisy's ears and out the other. As far as Daisy was concerned, their teaching was just garden fertilizer and didn't amount to a hill of beans.

Daisy, with her brown eyes and bubbly personality, made all the other veggies green with envy. Her parents, good Christians that they were, had always given reverence to Godfather Goodson and told her that he provided for them, but they sometimes made bad choices, which resulted in harsh consequences. They told her Godfather Goodson was trustworthy and faithful, and he always had their best interests at heart. Daisy knew little about him except that he was her caretaker, and he always made her roots feel good when he softened the soil around them. Daisy's mind was like a mixed salad because between the example set by her parents, the other marriages that were on skid row, and the information she got from through the grapevine, she thought it would be easier just to run away from home by climbing a beanstalk into heaven to find her fortune and true love. Her parents encouraged her to talk with Godfather Goodson about her problems and establish a relationship with him.

Be anxious for nothing, but in everything by prayer and supplication, with thanksgiving, let your request be known to God; and the peace of God, which surpasses all understanding, will guard your hearts and mind through Christ Jesus.

—Philippians 4:6–7 NKJV

They told her that Godfather Goodson had the ability to read minds and to know hearts. However, Daisy was a teenager; all she wanted to do was to read "happily ever after" stories, dream of her future with her sugarplum, and imagine their life together in their garden home. Daisy, however, knew the dangers of playing the field, and she didn't want to be canned and labeled as easy pickings, nor did she want to have cabbage patch children with a husband who would be a deadbeat dad. She didn't want one that wouldn't take an active role in their lives, or one that wouldn't pay cabbage (money/child support), or one that wouldn't hold a job to earn cabbage but would spend all day smoking (cabbage/tobacco), or worse, one that would become a weed head, who would spread germs by sharing pots with others.

Train up a child in the way he should go and when he is old he will not depart from it.

—Proverbs 22:6 NKJV

CHAPTER 3

Daisy's Suitors

Mr. Corn

Daisy had already been creamed by her first experience with courtship when she fell head over heels for Mr. Corn. Mr. Corn stood about six feet tall, and he was all ears but a poor listener. He was tall, dark, and handsome and, judging from the tassels he sported, well educated. At first glance, he gave the impression of being shy and modest—a man of few words. However, after a few sips from his nutritional drink, he seemed to buzz like a bee. His demeanor changed, and he became a corn dog and a beacon of knowledge. He claimed to have graduat-

ed with honors from Corn-Yell University. He boasted that he came from a family of kernels, and he was voted the world's most perfect vegetable. He was quick to boast of his ability to reduce the risk of colon cancer and anemia, improve bone strength, and control diabetes. Daisy, however, felt that a future with him would end in heartbreak because he made her feel small. He also had the irritating habit of ending all his statements with the word "shucks." She admired him for being an attentive father because he always had his children attached to his side, but she wondered: If she married him, would they be able to spend time together without the children? She also wondered how much time she would have to bond with her children if they were always attached to him. Daisy wanted more than to be his sidekick. She was also aware of problems associated with blended families and father-daughter attachment issues. Furthermore, in her heart, she knew he wouldn't be around, come the first frost.

A prudent man conceals knowledge, But the heart of fools proclaims foolishness.
—Proverbs 12:23 NKJV

Dead flies putrefy the perfumer's ointment, and cause it to give off a foul odor; So does a little folly to one respected for wisdom and honor.
—Ecclesiastes 10:1 NKJV

Mr. Cucumber

Daisy was impressed with Mr. Cucumber, especially with his athleticism. Mr. Cucumber claimed to have traveled the world. He was a champion athlete in five sports, but he excelled in track and field. He loved to flex his muscles, show his abs, and display his trophies. He claimed to have played in numerous super salad bowls and had won the most valuable player in each of them. Mr. Cucumber came from a family of creeping vines, which included watermelon, pumpkin, and cantaloupe. He was 95 percent water and good for hydration; he was rich in vitamins A and C and folic acid. He was good to treat skin problems, such as swelling of the eyes and sunburn, as well as protect from kidney stones. However, he was "cool as a cucumber," a ladies' man, quick to flex his muscles, even in casual conversations. Mr. Cucumber claimed he could lift a thousand grains. He was a very impressive specimen, but he was fickle and conceited with a one-track mind. He loved to hang out in salad bowls at parties, flirting with cabbages and other stationary vegetables. Daisy had a natural attraction to him, but she was bothered by the fact that his body naturally grew tendrils, which could attach to trellises and other supporting structures. His large leaf served as a canopy over his fruit. There were rumors that during the night, he had rescued many female veggies from fires using his ability to climb, his muscles, his water hose, and other things he concealed under his canopy. The lady veggies called him "a smooth operator." However, days after his rescues, he would find himself in a pickle with their boyfriends. Daisy noticed that even when he had nothing to climb, he sprawled along the ground for miles, claiming to be looking for employment. He returned home weeks later with a tan but without cabbage. Daisy felt that a relationship with him would end in heartbreak. She couldn't imagine herself in a relationship in which she would be a trophy wife.

Come, let us take our fill of love until morning; Let us delight ourselves with love. For my husband is not at home; He has gone on a long journey.

—Proverbs 7:18–19 NKJV

Mr. Onion

On the other hand, Mr. Onion was a crooner, who often tried to woo the female veggies by singing and playing songs on his guitar. The problem was, he could only play and sing one song, and it was a sad song. His song, "Looking for Love in Empty Spaces," would spoil a romantic moment and turn it into a tear party. Mr. Onion, however, would try to use it to his advantage by portraying himself as being misunderstood. He would gain the veggies' sympathy, then make them promises that he had no intention of keeping, leaving them disappointed, stewed, or stir fried. Some of the veggies complained of having allergic reactions to him, such as intense itching, blurred vision, asthma, or intense sweating. Although he was an excellent source of vitamin C and good for reducing the risks of Parkinson's, cardiovascular disease, and strokes, sometimes his negative attributes seemed to outweigh the positives. He had to be taken in small portions; needless to say, most of his relationships were short term.

Mr. Squash

The polar opposite of Mr. Onion was Mr. Squash. Mr. Squash was a politician, and Daisy had an instant attraction to him because of his vocabulary and his smooth talk. She was fascinated by the fact that he could say a lot with few words and use a lot of words to say nothing. What was more impressive about Mr. Squash was that he was running for the office of president of Field Town. He promised the veggies of Field Town that if elected, he would boost immune systems, manage diabetes, improve lung health, and serve in his anti-inflammatory capacity to reduce arthritis, gout, gastric ulcers, and improve cardiovascular systems. He promised to work with the other systems to pass bills that were rich in vitamins A and C and that the bills would contain minerals such as potassium, phosphorous, calcium, and iron. He promised there would be a vitamin in every pot. Daisy was fascinated by his smooth talk and could imagine herself being the first lady of Field Town.

Mr. Squash loved to debate, and his crooked neck gave him an advantage because he was stiff necked and hardheaded in all his opinions, mainly because he could only see one side of an issue. As a husband, however, Daisy thought he might be rigid and insensitive when it came to marital issues. She grimaced at the prospect of him driving their children to school. She became disillusioned with him when she researched his family tree and discovered that he was a fruit. *Imagine that!* she said to herself. *Presenting yourself as a vegetable when you are a fruit. What party are you in?* This is what she would mutter to herself as she further researched his family tree. The fact was that he was a vegetable, but he presented himself as a fruit because of his overlapping characteristics with fruit.

What bothered Daisy even more was when she discovered Mr. Squash was related to the pumpkin family. Being a part of the pumpkin family was frightful to Daisy because she knew that the pumpkin family carried dominant genes for obesity. She was also alarmed by the fact that the pumpkin family had the strange ritual of carving their faces in October, but in November they were as sweet as pumpkin pie. Daisy thought it was unethical for Mr. Squash to be running for office as a vegetable without revealing his fruitful past. She concluded that Mr. Squash was just a Crock-Pot and wondered what other secrets he wasn't revealing. She also learned that like Mr. Cucumber, Mr. Squash was a member of the creeping vine family, but unlike Mr. Cucumber, he lacked tendrils, would wilt quickly in the sun, and tended to travel in circles. Daisy couldn't imagine herself married to someone who couldn't be transparent in all areas of their relationship. Daisy fell into a depression because her dreams of becoming the first lady of Field Town—with all the fame, notoriety, and worthy causes she could champion—were squashed.

Mr. Zucchini

Mr. Zucchini was a cousin to Mr. Squash, but they were as different as night and day. Mr. Zucchini still lived with his parents. He was unemployed and spent most of the day playing garden games. He suffered from a garden disease called "failure to thrive." Mr. Zucchini loved to bully and play practical jokes on other veggies. He would trick them into participation in sports. Mr. Tomato played squash ball with him, which resulted in his being grilled and pasted. Mr. Tomato spent three months in the Greenhouse Hospital of Field Town recovering from his injuries. Mr. Pea had black eyes after playing table tennis with him. He even tried to trick Mr. Eggplant into playing baseball to use him as a catcher's mitt; needless to say, Mr. Zucchini spent time at the county jail of Field Town, trying to explain his intentions. In spite of his primitive interactions and lack of tact, Mr. Zucchini was voted the garden's most complete vegetable because he was richest in all nutrients and vitamins and was good for all body systems.

He who trusts in his riches shall fall, but the righteous will flourish like foliage.

—Proverbs 11:28 NKJV

CHAPTER 4

Daisy's Faith Journey

Daisy was tired of playing the dating game. She had discussions with her parents, but their advice seemed old fashioned. Daisy felt that they had a sour-grape marriage because sometimes when they argued, they blamed each other for their shortcomings. Daisy's father would say to her mother, "I had high ambitions before I met you. I could have been the president of the Cabbage Bank of Field Town, but after I met you, I settled for robbing food banks."

Her mother would reply, "Well, I didn't do cherry picking when I chose to marry you. I could have married Mr. Planter; he was a nut who became a college professor."

Daisy would spend her nights crying, praying, and longing for her true love. "There is a time and a season for all things under the sun" is what her parents would tell her. They would encourage her to read the biblical almanac written by Godfather Goodson. They suggested that she attend church. They told her that counseling with him could assist her in solving her problems. Daisy hadn't attended church since she was a seedling, so in some ways, this was a new experience. At church she was introduced to the pastor, Reverend Simon Holyfield. He was a spirited man. He preached about positive change through faith as he stood between the crack in the concrete in his pulpit. He told her she would know her mate from the fruit he bore. He encouraged her to be patient and said that it would produce hope. She discussed with him her infatuations with Mr. Corn, who carried his fruit on his side, and Mr. Cucumber, who concealed his fruit under his canopy, and also Mr. Squash, who pretended to be a vegetable but was actually a fruit.

Daisy didn't understand at that time, but Reverend Holyfield was talking about the Fruit of the Spirit.

But "the fruit of the Spirit is love, joy, peace, longsuffering, kindness, goodness, faithfulness, gentleness, self-control. Against such, there is no law."
—Galatians 5:22–23 NKJV

Walk in the Spirit, and you shall not fulfill the lust of the flesh.
—Galatians 5:16 NKJV

He told her of life lessons learned from the Garden of Eden. He also told her the story of the sower who sowed the seed. Although it seemed to be a difficult time in her life, her heart was being cultivated to receive the seed of faith. He told her when the seed of faith began to grow, she would grow spiritually, and her eyes would be open to spiritual things. Reverend Holyfield smiled as he whispered to her what he called "the secret to finding a helpmate." He told her to learn from Adam and Eve's mistake. Adam and Eve's marriage was indeed perfect until they disobeyed the instructions of Godfather Goodson and relied upon their senses by eating of the Fruit of the Tree of the Knowledge of Good and Evil. He told her that if they had obeyed (resisted temptation) and talked it over with Godfather Goodson, their obedience would have been counted for righteousness, and their eyes would have been opened to the spiritual things of God. They would have received spiritual gifts, and their union would have lasted forever. In looking for a helpmate, he said, you need to consult with Godfather Goodson and obey his instructions. His instructions were written in the biblical almanac, sometimes called the Holy Bible. Their disobedience undermined Adam and Eve's union as helpmates, and the seed of sin was planted in their hearts. As a result, the lust of the flesh, deceitfulness of riches, and pride of life took root.

Now the works of the flesh are evident, which are adultery, fornication, uncleanness, lewdness, idolatry, sorcery, hatred, contentions, jealousies, outbursts of wrath, selfish ambitions, dissensions, heresies, envy, murder, drunkenness, revelries, and the like of which I tell you beforehand just as I also in times past, that those who practice such things will not inherit the kingdom of heaven.
—Galatians 5:19–21 NKJV

He said that the secret to finding a helpmate starts with your relationship with Godfather Goodson. Daisy found herself talking to Godfather Goodson about Reverend Holyfield's sermons when he came out to care for her. She told him that she was starting to believe what Reverend Holyfield told her about faith and patience and that she was trying to make positive changes in her life.

So Jesus answered and said to them, Have faith in God...
—Mark 11:22 NKJV

One night in her misery, when her heart was at its heaviest, she abruptly stopped crying. Her heart cried out, "Oh my holy stars, I see!" It was as if a light had come on in her head, and her eyes and ears were opened to spiritual things. She understood what her parents were trying to get her to understand. She thought, "Life is a process; it's a faith journey. There are times and seasons for all things, and all I have to do is not be hardheaded and trust and follow Godfather Goodson's instructions."

Trust in the Lord with all your heart, And lean not on your understanding; In all your ways acknowledge Him, And he will direct your paths.
—Proverbs 3:5–6 NKJV

And we know that all things work together for good for those who love God, to those who are called according to His purpose.
—Romans 8:28 NKJV

Daisy discussed her epiphany with her parents. She surrendered her heart to Godfather Goodson's will for her life. Daisy asked him to fill her head with understanding and knowledge of his word. She vowed that in whatever decisions she made, she would seek his counsel. She began to look at potential mates from a different perspective—their spiritual attractiveness as opposed to their outward appearance. She even began to see her parents' marriage in a different light. Daisy thought, "As chaotic as my parents' marriage seems to be, their marriage wasn't a sour-grape marriage; it was a sauerkraut marriage!" They chose to marry each other, but Godfather Goodson's will was sovereign in their relationship. Their marriage was a faith journey that had stood the test of time. She thought, "Maybe married couples whose relationships have fermented can have benefits far beyond that of fresh cabbage." She had learned in her health class at school that sauerkraut produced probiotics (like her parents' teaching) and was the body's first defense against toxins and harmful bacteria (poor decision making). Sauerkraut was good at reducing stress, anxiety, and depression and at improving memory and maintaining brain health. Daisy thought, "In a sauerkraut marriage, trials are the soil in which faith grows."

Happy is the man who finds wisdom, And the man who gains understanding; For her proceeds are better than the profits of silver, and her gains than fine gold.

—Proverbs 3:13–14 NKJV

CHAPTER 5

Daisy's Choice~Based Spiritual Insight

One day when she least expected it, she fell in love with Mr. Elvis Curley Parsley. He was a thin man—a wimp to some and just plate dressing to others. The funny thing about it was that Daisy now saw him in a spiritual light. She remembered that even though they grew up on different rows of life in the garden, she sang "Row, Row, Row, Your Boat" with him as the rain came down, filling up the space between their rows. She recalled that they had sung "Shoo Fly, Don't Bother Me" in the garden school choir. What a beautiful, boisterous voice he had and quiet confidence when faced with overwhelming odds. She wondered why she never considered him for a mate. Judging from physical appearance, he had

numerous shortcomings, but spiritually he produced the fruit of the spirit. Daisy remembered the words from Reverend Holyfield's sermons; he called it a spiritual analysis for choosing a helpmate: do not look at the appearance or physical stature.

For the Lord does not see as man sees; for man looks at the outward appearance, but the Lord looks at the heart.

—1 Samuel 16:7 NKJV

The heart is deceitful above all things.

—Jeremiah 17:9 NKJV

Be not unequally yoked together with unbelievers.

—2 Corinthians 6:14 NKJV

Daisy remembered that Reverend Holyfield had cautioned against making decisions based on the lust of the flesh, the deceitfulness of riches, and the pride of life (as did Adam and Eve). He told them to be sure to understand what love was by reading the biblical almanac. He also told her that she would know the right mate by his fruit.

Mr. Parsley had a steadfast heart; he was a godly man, often misunderstood and unappreciated. He was full of nutrients (vitamins A, B, and C), rich in minerals, and good for the heart and mind. Even his name meant "rock celery." He played numerous bodily roles but was exceptionally positive for cardiovascular health and cancer prevention. Mr. Parsley was the complete package; he balanced nutrition between mind, body, and soul.

For who is God, except the Lord? And who is a rock, except our God?

—Samuel 22:32 NKJV

Therefore whoever, hears these sayings of Mine, and do them, I will liken him to a wise man who built his house on the rock.

—Matthew 7:24 NKJV

Daisy and Elvis Build the Foundation of Marriage

During their courtship, Daisy and Elvis attended church regularly, and on their dates, they prayed together: "Where two or three are gathered together in My name, I am there in the midst of them" (Matt. 18:20).NKJV They wanted faith to be the cornerstone of their relationship. They wanted the foundation of their garden home to be built on a rock-solid foundation—one that would stand the test of time—and they both wanted to be rooted in a personal relationship with Godfather Goodson. They knew their relationship would remain steadfast in storms, high winds, and floods and against anything or anybody who threatened their union. They had faith they could depend on the Rock of Ages. Through prayer and meditation, they formed a spiritual bond. Godfather Goodson told them to keep the Holy Spirit first in their marriage.

But seek first the kingdom of God and his righteousness,
and all these things shall be added to you.
—Matthew 6:33NKJV

He told them that they needed to honor their father and mother to receive spiritual blessings. After weeks of courtship, Elvis dropped to one knee and popped the question: "Daisy, you are the apple of my eye and my helpmate; will you marry me?"

Daisy, with tears of joy in her eyes, said, "I stew!" Elvis then put the carrots on her finger. Daisy's parents gave their blessings to the union.

Daisy and Elvis's Wedding

All of Field Town, including the butterflies, attended the marriage ceremony. At the wedding, Mr. Mustard Seed was the best man, and Miss Cauliflower was the maid of honor. Mr. Cucumber flirted with the bridesmaids, while Mr. Corn tried to impress them with his wealth of knowledge and achievements, and of course Mr. Onion cried. The exchange of vows between the bride and groom was special. The bride and groom held hands as they looked toward heaven as they recited their vows together in harmony:

I will love You, O Lord, my strength. The Lord is my rock, my fortress, and deliverer; My God, my strength, in whom I trust; My shield and the horn of my salvation, My stronghold. I will call upon the Lord who is worthy to be praised; so shall I be saved from mine enemies. (Psalm 18:1–3 NKJV)

Then they turned to each other and acknowledged their need the spirit of God to deal with the times and seasons of marriage. They admitted they both had sinful natures, but they would pray together and ask God to help them resist the temptations that might threaten their vows.

In all your ways acknowledge Him, and He shall direct your paths.
—Proverbs 3:6 NKJV

Reverend Holyfield then said, "If there be any here that can give a reason why this couple should not be married, speak now or forever hold your peace." When no one spoke, he said, "I now pronounce you husband and wife. Whom Godfather Goodson has joined together, let no man put asunder; be fruitful and multiply, and may the grace of our Lord be with you."

Thunder and lightning came from the skies as their lips met.

Mr. Elvis "Curley" Parsley and Miss Daisy Cabbage Head became two peas in a pod, united in the bonds of holy matrimony, on Good Friday 2022. They began a new season in their lives together rooted in faith.

Mr. and Mrs. Elvis Curley Parsley spent their honeymoon in Italy, where they pollinated their marriage. They were blessed with seven children during their seasons of marriage. They stayed strong in faith as they raised their children. Their first child was a boy, and they named him Simon Peter Holyfield Parsley. He was diagnosed with a drought disorder and with a-cute anemia. Since Daisy and Elvis's relationship was rooted in faith, they were confident that Godfather Goodson had some wonderful missions in store for their son's life. They smiled as Dr. Brock Broccoli wrote this prescription to them for the care of Simon Peter Parsley.

> ## Doctor's Orders
>
> Get plenty of rest. (Rest on the promises of Godfather Goodson.)
>
> Take plenty of fluids. ("I am the living water.")
>
> Eat a balanced diet. (Study the old and new biblical almanac.)
>
> Take your medicine. (Believe that "I am able.")
>
> Call me in the morning. (Remember to pray.)

Mrs. Daisy Cabbage Head Parsley would tell her friends, "Godfather Goodson has blessed me with a godly husband and a good father for our children, and best of all, after all these seasons of marriage, he still gives me butterflies."

Elvis to His Wife, Daisy, on Valentine's Day

Who can find a virtuous woman? For her worth is far above rubies. The heart of her husband safely trusts her. She will have no lack of gain. She does him good and not evil all the days of her life.

—Proverbs 31:10–12NKJV

Charm is deceitful, and beauty is passing, But a woman who fears the Lord, she shall be praised.

—Proverbs 31:30NKJV

And they lived together bonded in faith in Godfather Goodson's Garden, knowing that there would be challenges in their lives, but their relationship was built on the rock of ages.

CHAPTER 7

Veggie Soup

There are no right or wrong answers; use your imagination, and have fun. Project onto yourself, your partner, and your relationship or the one you would like to have. (In the role-reversal section, allow for other variables, such as age, financial differences, blended families, prior marriage, and unresolved issues.)

SECTION ONE

The Life of a Cabbage in Godfather Goodson's Garden

A. What circumstances create the urgency for Daisy to find a mate?

B. Where do you think Daisy gets her information about courtships?

C. What do you think Daisy's sister's married life is like with Mr. Spinach?

D. Do you think the incarceration of their children is reflective of their marriage?

Need to examine present life circumstances for yourself and mate. Explore the motivation for marriage / what makes a good relationship before marriage.

Food for thought:

_____

_____

_____

_____

_____

_____

_____

_____

_____

_____

_____

SECTION TWO

The Greatest Love Story Ever Told / The First Marriage

    A. Why do you think Daisy's parents felt it necessary to tell her the history of Adam and Eve?

    B. What are they trying to tell her about the perfect marriage?

    C. What are they trying to get her to understand about the nature of God?

    D. Do you think that there were nutritional/spiritual benefits in the garden?

Need to examine your / your partner's value system / religious beliefs / family history. Explore what your thoughts are about the institution of marriage. Is it different from your potential mate's?

Food for thought:

_____

_____

_____

_____

_____

_____

_____

_____

_____

_____

_____

_____

_____

_____

SECTION THREE

Daisy's Analysis of Potential Mates

1. Mr. Corn (tall, dark, handsome, and accomplished)

    A. What do you think may be marital issues associated with Mr. Corn?
    B. Do you think Mr. Corn is insecure? If so, why?
    C. What is the significance of Miss Cabbage Head feeling "looked down on" by Mr. Corn?
    D. Other than his children, what could Mr. Corn's attachments to his side represent?

Role reversal: Mr. Cabbage Head marries Miss Corn (a veggie cougar with five previous marriages). How may their roles differ depending on accomplishments?

Food for thought:

_____

_____

_____

_____

_____

_____

_____

_____

_____

_____

_____

_____

_____

_____

_____

_____

2. Mr. Cucumber (man of swag / ladies' man)

    A. Why do you think Daisy is naturally attracted to Mr. Cucumber?

    B. What do you think might be Mr. Cucumber's views toward marriage?

    C. What may need to happen for Mr. Cucumber to consider marriage?

    D. The lust of the flesh might motivate Mr. Cucumber; what might be Daisy's motivation?

What may be some of the issues if they marry?

Role reversal: Mr. Cabbage Head meets Miss Cucumber (veggie with a sultry past). Can either change the other?

Food for thought:

_____

_____

_____

_____

_____

_____

_____

_____

_____

_____

_____

_____

_____

_____

3. Mr. Onion (man of many prior marriages / a prisoner of love)

    A.   What symbolism is there in Mr. Onion's sad songs?

    B.   What is it about Mr. Onion that makes veggies believe his sad songs?

    C.   What can Mr. Onion do to make his relationships last longer?

    D.   What do you think the terms "stewed" and "stir fried" mean in terms of relationships.

Need for self-assessment: What went wrong in prior relationships? Are you over prior relationships? What baggage are you bringing into the new one?

Role reversal: Mr. Cabbage Head marries Miss Onion. Miss Onion marries Mr. Onion.

Food for thought:

_____

_____

_____

_____

_____

_____

_____

_____

_____

_____

_____

_____

_____

_____

4. Mr. Squash (successful, opinionated, charming)

   A. Metaphorically speaking, what would a relationship be like with a crooked-neck person, who travels in circles and withers easily resemble?
   B. How important is it to know your potential mate's ancestry before marriage?
   C. How could Mr. Squash's personality become an issue in the marriage?
   D. What skills or personality qualities may Miss Cabbage Head need to cope with Mr. Squash?

Role reversal: Miss Squash and Mr. Cabbage Head (age differences / motivation to compromise)

Food for thought:

_____

_____

_____

_____

5.   Mr. Zucchini (impulsive, unambitious, man-child)
    A.   How would Mr. Zucchini's personality and actions transfer into a marriage?
    B.   What forms of occupations would Mr. Zucchini best be suited?
    C.   What may need to happen to improve his suitable for marriage?
    D.   What could marital issues that may arise from being married to Mr. Zucchini?

Role reversal: Miss Zucchini and Mr. Cabbage Head

Food for thought:

_____

_____

_____

_____

_____

_____

_____

_____

_____

_____

_____

_____

_____

_____

_____

_____

_____

_____

SECTION FOUR

Daisy's Road of Spiritual Growth

A. What was Daisy's emotional state when she decided to attend church?
B. What is the significance of Mr. Goodson and Reverend Holyfield's tandem?
C. What is starting to develop in Daisy that leads to her epiphany?
D. Mr. Parsley has many of the same nutrients as the others. What makes him different from the others? What makes Daisy and Elvis compatible?

Food for thought:

_____

_____

_____

_____

_____

_____

_____

_____

_____

_____

_____

_____

_____

_____

_____

_____

SECTION FIVE

Daisy Receives Spiritual Insight into Choosing a Helpmate

A. Identify the lust of the flesh, the deceitfulness of riches, and the pride of life in Daisy and each of her potential suitors.

B. If Daisy had married either of the suitors, could she have had a successful marriage? Why or why not?

C. What happens to the lust of the flesh, the deceitfulness of riches, and the pride of life in a faith-based marriage?

D. What would be the role of God's sovereignty, grace, and mercy if Daisy's marriage were unsuccessful?

Food for thought:

_____

_____

_____

_____

_____

_____

_____

_____

_____

_____

_____

CHAPTER 8

Stirring the Marital Gumbo

A Man's Heart plans his way, But the Lord directs his steps.

—Proverbs 16:9NKJV

A study of couples and relationships in the Bible and obstacles they faced.
David and Bathsheba (story of adultery/murder/grace) 2 Sam. Chapter 11 NKJV
  Outcome: Their first son died, but after repentance and God's Grace, their second son (Solomon) became king of Israel.

Jacob with his four wives (favoritism of wives and children / jealousy between children / deception) Gen. 29–34 NKJV
  Outcome: The tribe of Judah came from Leah, one of the rejected wives. The tribe of Judah has lineage to King David and Jesus Christ.

Hosea and Gomer (unfaithfulness/adultery/redemption) Hos. 1–3 NKJV
  Outcome: Hosea gained a better understanding of the Israelites' relationship with God (he received his preaching degree through this tumultuous marriage).

The rebellion of David's son, Absalom against David (a house divided) 2 Sam. 12:1–23 NKJV
(Favorite son becomes the enemy: "A man's foe shall be those of his own household.")

Ruth and Boaz (class differences / redemption) Ruth 1–4 NKJV
    Outcome: From rags to riches (root of Jesse / the lion of Judah / lineage of Christ)

Jezebel and Ahab (greed/covetousness/murder) 1 Kings 16–23 NKJV
    Outcome: "Fret not thyself because of evildoers / fulfillment of prophecy"

Abraham and Sara (fulfillment of the promise of God / God's favor)
    Outcome: The father of nations (Justification through faith)

Joseph/Mary (the plan of God in action / hunted by King Herod / obedience through faith)
Matt. 1–3 NKJV The fulfillment of the prophecy told in Genesis (the Savior is born).

These marriages and circumstances are examples of how God's will is sovereign, despite our choices and worldly circumstances. The seed of faith can be sowed in even the most tumultuous relationship. God is just. He is able and willing to forgive our sins if we confess them and believe in him.

Is there anything too hard for God at his appointed time? The paste that holds all the different ingredients of the marital gumbo together and gives it flavor (salt) is faith; the fire is the Holy Spirit, and Christ is the Chef.

So let us not lose strength. Trust in the Lord, and he will lead you in his way.

Caution: Don't Confuse the Herbs of a Good Marital Stew

Emotional affair: The meeting of the minds of two emotionally needy people both longing to find solutions, something, or someone to fill the emptiness in their lives. It's a rejection of God as the answer or the "I am" in their lives. Emotional affairs can result in physical attractions and later sexual affairs. The classic symptom is when one person says to the other, "He/she understands me better than my spouse." The long-term effects, however, are emptiness, distrust, and guilt because only a relationship with God can fill the empty soul.

Spiritual intimacy: When you allow the spirit of God to dwell in your heart. It starts with giving reference to God in all you do, knowing that God is a spirit and that only he is worthy of praise and trust, which are in themselves spiritual.

Do not make your mate or potential helpmate your God.

Spiritual reflection / inviting God into your moment: Can you find some of the character flaws that are in the characters of *A Garden Love Story* in yourself? If so, these may be some of the areas that you may want to ask God to help you deal with (spiritual solution) prior to marriage. It is easier to see the character flaws in your mate after marriage and see him or her as the root of the problems in the marriage.

But be doers of the word , and not hearers only, deceiving yourselves.
For if anyone is a hearer of he word and not a doer, he is like a man observing his natural face in a mirror; for he observers himself, goes away, and immediately forgets what kind of man he was.
But he who looks into the perfect law of liberty and continues in it, and is not a forgetful hearer but a doer of the works, this one will be blessed in all he does.

—James 1:22–25 NKJV

And why do you look at the speck in your brother's eye but do not consider the plank in your own eye?

—Matthew 7:3 NKJV

CHAPTER 9

Parables in Pictures

Snapshots in Times and Seasons in the Lives of Believers

About the Parables in Pictures Photographs

The photographs feature an okra plant that grew between the blocks of concrete. My garden was planted about thirty yards from where this single okra grew. What was significant was that the okra appeared during a time in my life when I was going through marital and other life trials. The okra plant's origins were an enigma to me. In trying to determine its origin, many questions flooded my mind. I questioned whether I had dropped a seed that inadvertently fell between the blocks of concrete as I was preparing to plant my garden. What was the probability that a single seed would grow where there was limited soil? Then there was what I referred to as the okra metamorphosis; the plant seemed to change shapes and sizes in a short amount of time. I started to take pictures of the okra because I felt no one would believe me if I told them what was happening and because, in all my years of gardening, nothing like this had ever happened. I took photographs of the okra during different times of the day and under different weather conditions. I always wanted to get a photograph of a butterfly or wasp nestled in its blossom, but I could never get one to cooperate. A transformation was taking place right before my eyes in the pictures, but I didn't realize a transformation was also taking place in me. Unfortunately, I couldn't see it while it was happening but only after the change had taken place. I still had questions as to how it could produce such an abundant yield without my gardening skills. Since this was a phenomenon, I became fascinated by it and took more photographs. For a while, I even put a tomato cage over it to protect it from animals, but it soon outgrew the cage. The photographs provided for good conversation when I visited my family and friends. My family and friends could see that I was in emotional pain, and they wanted to help me. They would tell me things that they felt would comfort me, things like, "Trust God. Have faith. Wait on the Lord." To me, these were mere words; couldn't they see that I needed medicine or something tangible to ease my pain? I needed hope. Sometimes I would show my family and friends the photographs as a means of distraction, because although I needed their support, they repeated the same things about having faith and trusting God. I felt like a castaway or someone on a deserted island, miles of water separating me from the relief I needed.

As I thought about my circumstances, I reflected on the scripture about how Jesus had walked on water. He walked on the storms of life and demanded that the sea be still. I had read the Bible throughout my life and was familiar with the miracles of Jesus. I knew that in instances where he healed, he always talked about having faith. I didn't realize that in all my years of reading the Bible, somehow I had impersonalized the word of God as it related to me. In other words, Jesus healed them (the sick in the Bible)—people with withered hands, people with diseases, people who were possessed with evil spirits. Although I was in extreme emotional pain and was praying to God for help, in my mind, I wasn't really like one of them.

One night, while reading the Nelson Study Bible and other biblical literature, I looked through the photographs of the okra, and something miraculous happened! The words in the Bible took on a different meaning. They started to make sense! The comforting words that my family and friends had been telling me became a visual through the essence of the still photographs of the okra plant. In other words, I could see the substance, or essence, of the still photographs and could relate the essence of the photographs to Bible scriptures. It was as if the essence or the core meaning of the photographs were interpreting the scriptures. I started comparing the harsh conditions in which I thought the okra plant was growing to my perception of my circumstances. Shuffling through the photographs, I kept saying, "I see!" as I wept. I believe that at that moment, the Spirit of God moved me, and my eyes were opened to the spiritual things of God. I sensed a calmness that seemed to engulf me. I knew at that moment that I could trust God to handle my circumstances. I cried out, "Oh my God, I can see the invisible."

For since the creation of the world His invisible attributes are clearly seen,
being understood by the things that are made, even His eternal power and Godhead,
so that they are without excuse, because, although they knew God, they did not glorify Him as God, nor were thankful,
but became futile in their thoughts, and their foolish hearts were darkened.
—Romans 1:20–21NKJV

There were times after this revelation that I would read the Bible and look through the okra photographs and seem to be in a state of confusion. Then I would ask the Lord, "Why are you doing this to me?"

I say, then: Walk in the Spirit, and you shall not fulfill the lusts of the flesh.
For the flesh lusts against the Spirit, and the Spirit against the flesh: and these are contrary to one another, so that you do not do the things that you wish.
—Galatians 5:16–17NKJV

Then there were other times I would just study the Bible and look through the photographs with a sheepish grin on my face, with an occasional grunt as I read the scriptures. Yes, I was one of them! Since this experience, I can see the essence of faith in nature, and my collection of photographs has grown to over fifty. Praise God!

Pray and Persevere
OVER ADVERSITY, THROUGH FAITH

Then He said, "To what shall we liken the kingdom of God?
Or with what parable shall we picture it?"
—Mark 4:30 NKJV

For the Kingdom of God is not eating and drinking,
but righteousness and peace and joy in the Holy Spirit.
—Romans 14:17 NKJV

Perseverance

IN TIMES OF TROUBLE, HOPE TRIUMPHS BY FAITH THROUGH THE HOLY SPIRIT.

Therefore, having being justified by faith, we have peace with God through our Lord Jesus Christ, through whom also we have access by faith into this grace in which we stand, and rejoice in hope of the glory of God. And not only that, but we also glory in tribulations, knowing that tribulation produces perseverance; and perseverance, character and character, hope.

—Romans 5:1–4 NKJV

PEACE CAN BE FOUND IN JESUS.

"These things I have spoken to you, that in Me you may have peace. In the world you* will have tribulation; but be of good cheer, I have overcome the world."

—John 16:33 NKJV

"Abide in Me, and I in you. As the branch cannot bear fruit of itself, unless it abides in the vine, neither can you, unless you abide in Me."

—John 15:4 NKJV

Oasis

GOD'S GOODNESS IS FOUND IN DRY AND DIFFICULT CIRCUMSTANCES.

I spread out my hands to You; My soul *longs* for You like a thirsty land.

—Psalm 143:6 NKJV

Faith as a mustard seed

—Matthew 17:20 NKJV

Jesus said to him, *"If you can believe, all things are possible to him who believes."* —Mark 9:23 NKJV

...Two blind men followed Him crying out and saying, "Son of David have mercy on us!"...And Jesus said to them, *"Do you believe hat I am able to do this?"..."According to your faith let it be to you"* and their eyes were opened... —Matthew 9:27–30 NKJV

But without faith it is impossible to please *Him*, for he who comes to God must believe that He is a rewarder of those who diligently seek Him. —Hebrews 11:6 NKJV

The Origins of Faith
(THE ESSENCE OF FAITH)

A cry in distress
(Matt. 14:29–30)

A voice
(Ps. 95:6–8)

A touch
(Matt. 14:34–36)

A prayer
(Dan. 9:21)

A glimpse
(Luke chapter 19

A belief
(Mark 9:23

A wait
(Ps. 27:14)

A confession
(Rom. 10:8–9)

Faith as a mustard seed... —Matthew 17:20

Now faith is the substance of things hoped for,
the evidence of thing not seen. —Hebrews 11:1

A CONFIDENCE 2 Cor. 5:6

For we walk by faith, not by sight. —2 Corinthians 5:7

*All scriptures NKJV

Born Again

But your iniquities have separated you from your God; And your sins have hidden His face from you, So that He will not hear. —Isaiah 59:2 NKJV

"I have come that they may have life, and that they may have it more abundantly" —John 10:10 NKJV

And you *He made alive*, who were dead in trespasses and sins, in which you once walked according to the course of this world, according to the prince of power of the air, the spirit who now works in the sons of disobedience, among whom also we all once conducted ourselves in the lust of the flesh, fulfilling the desires of the flesh and of the mind, and were by nature children of wrath, just as the others. —Ephesians 2:1–3 NKJV

For if we have been united together in the likeness of His death, certainly we also shall be *in the likeness of His resurrection*, knowing this, that our old man was crucified with Him, that the body of sin might be done away with, that we should no longer be slaves of sin. —Romans 6:5–6 NKJV

The Sower and the Seed

Listen! Behold, a sower went out to sow. —Mark 4:3 NKJV

The sower sows the word...the word is sown in the heart. —Mark 4:14–15

<u>**Some seeds fell by the wayside, some on stony ground,**</u>
<u>**some on thorny ground.**</u>
Heart conditions
Wicked heart (Prov. 26:3), Grieving heart (Ps. 73:21),
Hard heart (Ps. 59:8), Proud heart (Ps. 101:5),
Confused heart (Deut. 28:28), Doubting heart (James 1:6),
Haughty heart (Ps. 13:11), Heart in turmoil (Job 30:27),
Dull heart (Isa. 6:10), Evil heart (Gen. 5:5)

- Satan takes away the seed, receives but no depth / no root
- Cares of the world / deceitfulness of riches
- Lack of understanding
- Lack of endurance / moisture
- Prefers praise of men over praise of God

<u>**Some fell on good ground:**</u>
Willing Heart Ex. 35:22
Yearning heart Job 19:27
Steadfast heart (Ps. 57:7)
Broken heart Ps. 34:18
Sincere heart Eph. 6:5
Pure in heart Matt. 5:8

- Hears, accepts, understands through faith
- Confession, repentance, surrender: "Thy will be done"

But the Lord said to Samuel, "Do not look at his appearance or physical stature because I refused him. For the Lord does not see as man sees; for man looks at the outward appearance, but the Lord looks at the heart." —1 Samuel 16:7

...Is there anything too hard for God at his appointed time? —Genesis 18:14

"But these are the ones sown on good ground, those who hear the word, accept it, and bear fruit; some sixty and some a hundred." —Mark 4:20

The sacrifices of God are a broken spirit, A broken and contrite heart—These O, God, You will not despise. —Psalm 51:17

Create in me a clean heart, O God, And renew a steadfast spirit within me.
—Psalm 51:10

*All scriptures NKJV

Trust

WE CAN TRUST AN OMNISCIENT GOD FOR THE UNKNOWN FUTURE.

Notice the trees in the autumn season (as indicative of the colors of the leaves). However, the okra appears to be in the spring season (as evident by the green foliage). The trees are probably over thirty years old. The okra is seasonal (and planting season is in summer). It thrives, even though it seems to be in the wrong season and under adverse conditions.

Things Are Not Always What They Seem; Only God Knows What's Going on behind the Scenes: The Story of Job

LIFE IS HARD

(Life circumstances)

GOD IS GOOD!

(Mustard Seed faith)

A Life of **FAITH** Is Lived between the Two Realities

Caught Between a Rock and a Hard Place?

GOD'S GRACE IS ABLE TO SUSTAIN YOU AND PROVIDE FOR ALL YOUR NEEDS.

Trials Are the Soil in Which Faith Grows

(PROFITING FROM LIFE'S TRIALS)

My brethren, count it all joy when you fall into various trials, knowing that the testing of your faith produces patience.

—James 1:2–3 NKJV

Notice how the wind is tossing the leaves of the plant; however, the stalk anchors it between the crack in the concrete, and it remains strong despite its circumstances. After the storm it will emerge stronger. You could say that it was just getting its spiritual exercise.

The Thorn in the Flesh:
STRENGTH THROUGH WEAKNESS

Concerning this thing I pleaded with the Lord three times that it might depart from me. And He said to me, *"My grace is sufficient for you, for My strength is made perfect in weakness."* Therefore most gladly I will rather boast in my infirmities, that the power of Christ may rest upon me. Therefore I take pleasure in infirmities, in reproaches, in needs, in persecutions, in distresses, for Christ sake. For when I am weak, then I am strong.
—2 Corinthians 12:8–10 NKJV

God uses human weakness to reveal his great sufficiency, so if he works through us, his power we will see. **<u>To experience God's strength, we must recognize our weaknesses.</u>**

The Dynamics of Faith.

HEALING THE WOMAN WITH THE HEMORRHAGE:

Now a certain woman had a flow of blood for twelve years, and had suffered many things from many physicians. She had spent all that she had and was no better, but rather grew worst. When she heard about Jesus, she came behind Him in the crowd and touched His garment. For she said, "if only I may touch His clothes, I shall be made well." Immediately the fountain of her blood was dried up, and she felt in her body that she was healed of the affliction. And Jesus immediately knowing in Himself that power had gone out of Him, turned around in the crowd and said, "Who touched my clothes?" But His disciples said to Him, "You see the multitude thronging You and You say, "Who touched Me?" And He looked around to see her who had done this thing. But the woman, fearing and trembling, knowing what had happened to her, came and fell down before Him, and told Him the whole truth. And He said to her, "Daughter, your faith has made you well go in peace and be healed of your affliction." —Mark 5:25–34 NKJV

The photograph: The okra plant appears to be in an impossible situation. It is growing between the cracks in the concrete. The woman with the hemorrhage also seem to be in an impossible situation. She had an illness for twelve years and had sought assistance from physicians. She had spent all her money to find a cure, only to find that the sum of her efforts resulted in her illness getting worst. The trees in the background are symbolic of the autumn season (as evidenced by the color of the leaves). The woman with the hemorrhage was also in her autumn season of health (broke, sick, and without hope). Notice how the okra plant had already produced a harvest, but it seems to be in spring and is about to produce another harvest. The trees are in autumn, and the okra is in spring, although they are fewer than ten yards apart. The trees are in their natural environment and will be there year round. The okra plant is in an unnatural environment and is not expected to return next season. The woman with the hemorrhage was about to enter a new season, a season of faith and healing. The leaves in the photograph are symbolic of emptiness, hopelessness, or pending death felt by the woman. There is, however, a force (faith) that accounts for the two seasons. The force activated the Holy Spirit (power) was the healing power that left Jesus's body. By faith the woman with the hemorrhage went from a season of death and despair to one of faith and healing.

Description of faith:

Now faith is the substance of things hoped for, the evidence of things not seen. —Hebrews 11:1NKJV

Faith is the medium in which the Holy Spirit moves.

Combining the story of the woman with the hemorrhage with the description of faith and the essence of faith in the photograph, you arrive at this scripture:

Jesus said to her, "I am the resurrection and the life. He who believes in Me though he may die he shall live And whosoever lives and believes in Me shall never die, Do you believe this?" She said to Him, "Yes Lord, I believe that You are the Christ, the son of God, who is to come into the world." —John 11:25–27 NKJV

CHAPTER 10

Souped-Up—Cabbage Head Exam

1. Using the story of Daisy Cabbage Head and the parable of The Sower And The Seed (Mark chapter 4), can you follow the stages of Daisy's spiritual growth (heart cultivation) Using the photograph of The Sower And The Seed from page 60? Can you apply the photograph of the sower and the seed to your spiritual growth?

2. Can you relate the Pictures in the Parables section to difficult circumstances in your life (marital or otherwise) that you have been able to overcome or had to accept God's sovereignty ("Thy will be done") in the situation?

3. How do the photographs, *Faith as a Mustard Seed and The Origins of Faith (photographs on pages 57 and 58 respectively)*, relate to Daisy's faith journey? Can you relate them to your faith journey?

4. How does the photograph *Oasis* relate to God's sovereignty, his ability to provide for needs in any life situation or hardship?

5. Notice that the photograph of *Trust* (page 61) and the photograph of *The Dynamic of Faith: Healing the Woman with the Hemorrhage* (page 66) are the same. What does it say about the correlation between trusting God and having faith in God in terms of a relationship with him?

6. What do you think is the correlation between the *Perseverance* photograph on page 54 and the *Life Is Hard, but God Is Good* photograph on page 62?

7. Metaphorically speaking, have you ever been "CAUGHT BETWEEN A ROCK AND A HARD PLACE"? If so, tell your story as you look at the photograph by the same name on page 63.

8. Do a study of the Parables in Pictures photographs by taking each photograph and reading the full chapter of the Bible scriptures associated with it. Does the visual enhance the meaning of the scripture or chapter?

9. Can you relate the *Trials Are the Soil in Which Faith Grows* photographs (page 64) to Matthew 8:23–27 NKJV (The wind and waves obey Jesus)?

10. Do you think that all the characters (with exceptions of Reverend Holifield and Godfather Goodson), may be on their own faith journeys, although they appear to have different life circumstances?

Bonus exercise: Brainstorm ways from a scientific perspective of how the one seed of okra got between the crack of concrete (since it wasn't put there purposely) and reasons why it shouldn't have been able to survive its circumstances. Brainstorm ways from a spiritual perspective of how the seed of okra may have gotten between the concrete and why was it able to prosper.

Food for thought:

_____

_____

_____

_____

_____

_____

_____

God Speaking to Man through Nature

- Moses at the burning bush Exodus chapter 3 NKJV
- The budding rod of the Levites (Aaron) Num. 17:1–10; Heb. 9:4 NKJV
- Pharaoh and the plagues Exod. 7–11, NKJV
- Jesus cursed the fig tree Matt. 21:18, NKJV
- The dreams of Joseph Gen. 37:5–9, NKJV
- Joseph interprets Pharaoh's dream Gen. 40:1–23, NKJV
- Balaam, the donkey, and the angel / the donkey speaks Num. 22:28, NKJV
- The signs shown to Gideon(Judg. 6:36–40, NKJV)
- The tempest / Jesus and the disciples on board a ship Matt. 8:23–26, NKJV
- The dividing of the Red Sea Exod. 14:19–30, NKJV
- Jonah and the fish/plant/worm Jon. 1:17, 4:5–11, NKJV
- Paul on the road to Damascus (the sun) Acts 9:3–19, NKJV
- The voice of Cain's blood crying out to God from the ground Gen. 4:10, NKJV
- Natures reaction to JesusChrist giving up the ghost on the cross Matt. 27:50–53, NKJV

The heavens declare the glory of God; And the firmament His handiwork.

—Psalm 19:1 NKJV

The Holy Spirit Moves through Faith
STORIES OF FAITH AND SOVEREIGNTY

The crack in the concrete (the heart of man), is where the seed of faith is sown. The Holy Spirit of God moves, and God's power is displayed to the unbeliever, the lost, the confused, and the defiant. When the Holy Spirit moves, lives are transformed, leaders (Paul) become servants, shepherds (David) become conquerors, cowards (Gideon) become mighty men; the defiant (Jonah) become prophets, and the rejected (Jesus) become king. There may come a season of trials in your life when you are confronted with circumstances beyond your control or trials that are the results of poor choices. The trials expose your vulnerabilities, and you may ask yourself, "Why me?" This is the sower's good season; the heart is being cultivated to receive the seed of faith. Through faith, the Holy Spirit moves, and spiritual healing and transformation will take place according to the will of God. God is refining you through your trials to be a vessel to himself. Pray the prayer of faith—"Thy will be done"—and meditate on his word.

And the Lord said to Abraham, "Why did Sarah laugh, saying "shall I surely bear a child, since I am old? " Is anything too hard for the Lord? At the appointed time, I will return to you, according to the time of life, and Sarah shall have a son."
—Genesis 18:13–14 NKJV

Displaced?

Our heavenly father knows how to care for his children and will only allow what he deems best. We can rest in his infinite wisdom and goodness.

Honey!.... Who put the Barbecue Grill In The Garden?

My flesh and my strength fail; but God is the strength of my heart and my portion forever.

—Psalm 73:26 NKJV

ABOUT THE AUTHOR

Charlie L. Jones, Licensed Independent Clinical Social Worker (LICSW)

Charlie L. Jones was born in Tuscaloosa, Alabama, and received both his bachelor's degree in communications and his master's degree in social work from the University of Alabama. He has over thirty years of experience in the mental health field, ranging from being a case manager to running an independent private practice.

When counseling couples using a Christian approach to problem solving, he often incorporates photographs from nature as a therapeutic tool. Many of Jesus's teachings through parables involved nature. The photographs can have a calming effect, and they often facilitate points of mutual agreement. After "retirement" he returned to the field of social work as an outpatient drug treatment therapist.

Charlie spends time gardening and studying the word of God, and through prayer, meditation, and faith, he has found a sense of purpose. He has an exhibit of photographs from nature called *The Parables in Pictures Photograph Collection*. He enjoys writing and is the author of *Growing a Successful Marriage through Faith*, which is available on Amazon.com.

Printed in the USA
CPSIA information can be obtained
at www.ICGtesting.com
LVHW070335041023
760080LV00003B/72